SHTF Prep

Preppers

MW01244300

SHTF

(2 in 1)

Book 1
SURVIVAL

A Beginners Guide to Survive

Table of Contents

Introduction

Prepping: Getting Started

Setting Up The Pantry

Your Emergency Survival Bag

Making Provisions For Water

How To Purify Water

Sourcing For Food

Tips On How To Identify Edible Food During Foraging

Hunting And Setting Traps For Survival

Setting Up A Survival Shelter

How To Set Up A Survival Shelter

How To Make A Fire Without A Matches Or Lighter

Survival Defense Techniques

How To Outsmart Wildlife

Conclusion

Introduction

I want to thank you and congratulate you for downloading the book, *"SURVIVAL - A Beginners Guide to Survive"*.

This book contains actionable information on how to survive in any unfortunate situation.

Have you ever thought of how you could live if you were faced with a life-threatening emergency? Although nobody is praying or hoping for a life threatening event to happen, we know that these events happen all the time. For instance, what if you are caught up in a natural disaster? What if you get lost in a bush land or an island so far away from your home? What if there was a war, or a catastrophic natural disaster that displaced you only to find yourself in a far away area away from home and anyone you know? Or what if you get lost in a desert? What will your next course of action be? Will you sit there and bemoan your fate while waiting for death to take you?

As I mentioned earlier, nobody is hoping for such disasters, but just to be on the safe side, it is better to get prepared for the occurrence of such events to help you survive if such an event occurs. Well, if you've ever thought about it or just thought about it and are looking for information on how to survive if disaster were to strike, this book has the information you need to stay alive and well.

This book will cover issues like; setting up your bag out bag and pantry, how to source for water in the wild, how to search for food to survive and various things you can eat to survive. You will also learn about providing shelter for yourself, how to tell time without a watch and finally some defense techniques you need to defend yourself from wild animals and other predators. After reading this book, you will be ready to start implementing what you will have learnt when going in your next camping trip.

Thanks again for downloading this book, I hope you enjoy it!

Wait! Before you start reading click here to check out your FREE bonus before it's to late!

If you enjoy learning about Prepping and Survival than check out my other titles

PREPPER

No 1 Survival Guide Book For Prepper's

SURVIVAL

Survival Pantry, a Prepper's guide to Storing food and water

Prepping: Getting Started

When disaster strikes, many of us hope that the government will be there to help. And it does. But one thing is true; even with all the budgetary allocation for disaster preparedness, when disaster strikes, the victims face it first hand and before any help can show up, you will probably have spent several hours, days or even weeks before help can come depending on where you are and the nature of the disaster. Well, unfortunately, that's how life is and in as much as we may want to say that the government might fail in its responsiveness, it may not be practically possible to help everyone when disaster strikes especially when the area affected is pretty large and is densely populated. And even if you were to go to your nearby rescue center, the truth is that they may be pretty ill prepared for an emergency thus making it almost impossible for them to manage the large group of those in need. Soon, you will start fighting for staples when the rescue center cannot keep up with the number. So what should you do at such times? Well, if you were not prepared, the best thing you can hang on is hope. But when you start prepping, you have control over what happens during a survival situation. You don't just wait for the government and aid agencies to rescue you. Instead, you take deliberate measures to ensure that you have everything you need to survive. But even with all the prepping, one thing is true; your mindset is your biggest asset when it comes to prepping. With the right mindset, you can do anything and overcome any challenge you may face. But whatever you do, it is important to keep in mind that:

- 3 minutes without air is enough to leave you unconscious

- 3 hours without synchronized body temperature is enough to leave you unconscious

- 3 days without water will leave you dead

- 3 weeks without food is enough to kill you

This means one thing; as you prepare for survival, you need to make sure that you prep in order i.e. shelter followed by water then finally food. With proper planning, assessment, and re-evaluation, you should be able to avoid/minimize panic and negative mindset and with that, your chances of survival will be drastically increased. So how do you prep? Where do you start? Well, it starts with preparing a survival pantry. Let's learn how to do that in the next chapter.

Setting Up The Pantry

Without food and water, you are pretty much doomed no matter what else you may be having. As such, before you can do anything else, the first thing you need to do is to set up a survival pantry (you can keep this in a survival bag or in a fixed pantry in your house) where you will keep enough food to sustain you for a few days into the disaster. For this, you will need to consider the perceived impact and the period you think the disaster may last. Don't just stockpile stuff that you have never eaten. Instead, stock stuff that you eat daily to avoid instances of discovering that you cannot eat something after wasting all the space and energy to keep a certain food. Nonetheless, what you pack in your pantry (or survival bag) is truly up to you but as you do that, you need to consider a few pointers:

Macronutrients: You should aim to have all the essential macronutrients in your pantry to ensure that you have a balanced meal. This should ideally comprise 5-20% proteins for toddlers & babies, 10-35% proteins for adults, and 10-30% proteins for kids and teens. As for carbs, you should aim for about 45-65% and for fats; you should aim to have 30-40% for babies & toddlers, 25-35% for kids & teens, and 20-35% for adults. As for the calories, you should aim for at least 1200 calories.

Tip about meals: Aim for about 500-700 calories per meal for each of the three meals then calculate that for the number of days that you want the food to last you. To help you stockpile fast, try to buy an extra item every time you go shopping. You will soon find yourself with a good quantity of such items. But don't just keep them forever; try to cycle such items in your everyday consumption to ensure you don't end up with expired food products. You can try to keep the new food at the back and those that have stayed for awhile at the front.

Tip: Keep in mind that there is something referred to as food fatigue caused by taking the same old food every other day. As such, don't just assume that any food is food during a survival situation. Try to have variety if you truly want to have a smooth time. You can pack such things like:

45-60 ready to eat meals packed in vacuum pouch bags.

Salt and pepper to make food tasty

Seeds: these are easy to pack and are light to carry around. Of course, if you are to survive in the wild for longer, you will somehow need to figure out a way of growing your own foods and not just relying on fish and meats. You can pack squash, corn, tomatoes, cantaloupe, lettuce, early carrots, broccoli, watermelon, Swish chard, onions, red beets, pumpkins, potatoes (white), cabbage, spinach, various herbs, sweet potatoes etc.

Grains

These will be made up of energy giving food and they include; pasta, rice, oats, cereals, pancake mixes, stuffing mixes and other similar foods.

Vegetables

These will serve as your major source of vitamins and minerals and they include a variety of canned vegetables.

Fruits

You can get additional fruit supply through foraging, but you need to pick your own fruits just in case. Items in this category will include all canned fruits and fruit juice that come in containers.

Protein

Basic food in this category include; canned salmon, canned tuna, peanut butter, canned lentils, canned legumes, canned soups, eggs and dried legumes.

Diary Food

These are other sources of proteins that will be needed and they will include packed dry milk, cheese, and yoghurt, canned liquid milk, soy milk etc.

Other Items

These are other miscellaneous items you will need in your survival bag and they include wine especially non-alcoholic ones because you will need to stay alert at all times to survive during this period. Others you will need will include: condiments like sauce, olive oil, butter, vinegar, ketchup, salt, ginger, pepper, dried herbs, sugar, and honey.

Tips For Stocking Your Bag

✓ Stick To Canned Items

You should always stick to canned items unless you are sure that your stay is a very short one. Canned foods can last for months if not years before they expire. That is the best option for you, not fresh foods that will get spoiled in a matter of days.

✓ Dried Items

You should always choose dried food to fresh ones; the moisture in dried foods has been extracted making them to last longer than fresh food.

✓ Think Long Term

You have to think long term when packing your pantry bag because you never can tell how long you will stay out there before help comes your way. So you need to include as many items as you can carry to last for a long time.

✓ Always Check For Expiration Dates

If you're buying canned food, it is advised that you take time to check the expiration dates for every item before purchase. Try to go for items with longer expiration dates.

✓ Balanced Meal

When packing your survival bag, ensure that the food in the bag is able to make you a balanced meal without your secondary source of food. That is why from the list I made on how to pack a pantry bag, I ensured that all the classes of food were present in the list to some extent. You need well balanced meals to stay fit, and fortify your immune system.

Important Note:

Even as you pack various foods, ensure to carry cookware; you can use a backpacker's cooking set, which you can fasten to the outside of the bug out bag or on your belt. But as you do this, ensure to carry one fork, a table knife and a strong spoon. You should also think of having a thick iron skillet or a cooking pot if need be.

Keep in mind that fire is life when it comes to survival. It will keep you warm at night and will help you prepare various foods comfortably. As such, don't under pack when it comes to prepping for fire because without anything else, knowing how to light a fire can keep you alive since you can hunt, catch various insects and prepare various foods. As such, ensure to have such things like 3 steel flint fire starters, bic lighters, waterproof matches and a hand lens.

And even as you do all that, you will also need to set up a survival bag i.e. the bug out bag that you will be carrying around with you or even place one at different places like in your car, your office, your home and other areas just to ensure that you always have enough survival stuff to survive for several days if disaster strikes.

Your Emergency Survival Bag

Although disasters strike when least expected, you can go a long way to save your life when disaster strikes by having a survival kit prior to the occurrence of the event. A survival kit is a bag where you put basic items you will need for survival during an emergency until help comes your way (enough to sustain you for at least 3 days). That probably explains why most survival kits are light and easy to carry with you.

Water: Ensure to have at least 3 liters of water in your survival bag. This should be enough to sustain you for 3 days. Ensure to have water purification tablets, water storage bottle or bag, water filtration bottle for treating all kinds of water, and purification straw for treating free flowing water.

Clothes: get a strong pair of shoes, a cap, pants, towel, shirts, windcheater, and undergarments to survive with for at least 3 days. The clothes you keep will depend on the survival situation you are prepping for as well as the climate. Simply ensure to have the right clothes for the potential disaster.

Shelter: Ensure that you have a tent or a tarpaulin in your survival bag. Another thing you can have is a light sleeping bag or preferably bothy bag (for shelter) or a bedroll.

Food: Ensure to have enough food (mainly canned or dried). You can opt for survival rations, energy tablets and ration heaters (for heating frozen foods)

First aid items: Have enough supplies for dealing with all kinds of injuries. In a survival situation, all manner of injuries will be present. As such, don't just have the simple first aid kit; go for something more advanced. For instance, your first aid kit should contain a suction pump to pump out poisonous venom, splint, cotton wool, needle and thread, Hydrogen peroxide or liquid spirit and some tablets. Others you can have include SAM splint (for immobilizing limbs), first aid kit (for treating minor injuries), burns dressings (for soothing and protecting burns), haemostatic powder (for preventing excessive bleeding, wound closing plasters, insect protector (insect repellents and coverings and sun protection (cream and lotion).

Utensils and containers: you need a cooking pot for preparing meals, for doubling as cups and plates and probably storing/purifying water. Also, try getting

Fire making equipment: Ensure to have gasoline lighters (opt for the windproof option) waterproof matchbox etc. You should also ensure to have candles in your bag. You will also need to pack tinder (to help you start fire in any condition) and a flint for creating sparks under any condition.

Tools: In essence, you need to have such items like a survival knife, scissors, nylon rope, folding stick, hook, cutter, flashlight, batteries etc. You will also need compass for finding your way around. You will also need a saw for cutting wood and plastics, an axe for splitting wood, a small towel for digging mud and debris, and a crowbar for opening jammed windows and doors.

For lighting: Ensure to have a backup torch i.e. a pen torch, light sticks i.e. one time use glow sticks, hand torch for signaling through lighting and a head torch for keeping your hands free.

For heating and cooking: Ensure to have mess tins for cooking and heating on campfire, aluminum foil for minimal cooking, fuel depending on the stove, hexi stove, which is a stove that runs on solid fuel and solid fuel kettle if you have enough space.

For doing repairs: You can use a fishing line, sewing needle with thread, steel or brass wire, cable ties for repairing and binding, steel/brass wire for repairing and snaring, duct tape for fixing anything, nylon utility cord or paracord; you should have at least an item made with Paracord, either a bracelet or belt because a Paracord is very essential for your survival.

For battery: ensure to have alkaline batteries (AA or AAA), lithium batteries for the cold weather, solar charger that can charge batteries or charge devices, emergency charger for mobile and other devices etc.

Signaling and navigation: You can have the following items: Bright red jacket for warmth and signaling, mirror for camping and signaling, whistle without pea design that will not freeze, beacon i.e. a waterproof flashlight for signaling, compass for finding your way around and a satellite device whether it is a tracker or a satellite phone.

Communication devices: You can use a satellite phone, walkie talkie and radio

Note: Ensure that your survival bag is waterproof. Also, as you put stuff in your survival bag, it is important to remember that different survival situations will sometimes call for you to keep different things in your survival bag. For instance, the stuff you will keep when prepping for a flood or tsunami will definitely differ from what you will keep when prepping for a stay in a dessert. As such, you need to picture the scenario of what you will need in the particular situation that you are prepping for. You can add other items based on what you think you may need, but these are the basic items for survival you will need in case of emergency.

As you know very well, the stuff you will keep in your survival bag can only sustain you for so long. If you are to survive, you really need to ensure that you have all the information you need and probably practice how to live in the wild by scouting for water, food, making shelter and others. The rest of the book will focus on just that.

Making Provisions For Water

Water is one of the very important things you need to survive during an emergency. In fact I will keep water on top of my list because you can survive without other things like food for a longer period of time, but you cannot go without water for long. It may not come as a surprise to you that you can stay for 3 weeks which is approximately 21 days without food and still survive, but you can't survive without water for 3 to 4 days. This is to show you how important water is to your survival. So the question now is; how do you scout for water, or how will you make provisions for water when you are stranded in a desert or in an island?

Some of the ways you can source for water during an emergency include:

✓ **Rain Water**

If you are stranded in a desert, then this option may not be for you as it is very unlikely for rain to fall in a desert place. You can skip to other options mentioned below. Rainwater comes in handy in an emergency situation, especially if you are stranded in a bush land. You can look around for a small container (your survival bag should have pots, bottles and other containers) to collect water when it is raining or you can use a large leaf. To collect water using a leaf roll the leaf to give it a cone shape, fold the side you are holding and use the upper side of the leaf to collect raindrops. You can only use the second method to collect water which you will drink immediately because you can't save water using a leaf.

✓ **Look For Streams/Waterfalls**

Another method you can use is to walk around your surroundings to search for a nearby stream or waterfall. A stream or waterfall will take care of your drinking and bathing needs and it is actually the best option but if there isn't any stream near you, you can still use other methods. Ensure that your trip to scout your surrounding is done during the daytime when you can see clearly to avoid running into danger. Also, if you can't swim, remember to only use the riverbed.

When going on such a trip, you have to find a way of keeping track of your surroundings to avoid getting lost again. You can make marks on tree trunks as you go, or you can pick heavy stones and drop as you go or even tie twine on shrubs as you go.

Telltale Signs That A River Is Nearby

- Sound Of Rushing Water

The first sign that there is a river or stream nearby is that you will hear a sound of rushing water. All you need to do is to stand still and listen for the sound in the background. It might not always be a sound of rushing water; it can be a trickling sound if the water isn't fast moving.

- Via The Presence Of Some Insects

Some insects usually stay near water bodies and seeing them around means that there is a pool of water nearby. The most popular of them all is mosquitoes. Look out for mosquitoes in your environment; it's a sign that there is water not far from where you are.

- Birds can also signal where water is

Follow the direction towards which birds fly in the evening and in the morning.

- Damp Soil

Is the soil around the area damp? If yes, then it means that there is a stream or river nearby.

- Cool Temperature

Is the area cool? If the place is generally cool than other parts of the bush land, then it may be a sign that there is a waterfall nearby.

Also, look out for tracks of wildlife and lush green vegetation since this is a sign of nearby water. A muddy area is also a sign that there is water. Simply dig a hole then strain the water using a cloth

✓ Look For A Dry River Bed

A dry river bed can provide water for you, as some riverbeds still bring out water if you dig a shallow hole on it. If you see a riverbed around you, you can bore a hole with a strong stick (or use the hand shovel in your bug out bag) to see if you can get water from there. A dry riverbed is very easy to notice, because the ground looks all cracked up, while the soil is kind of moist if you dig into the soil.

✓ Soil Still Water

This method can be used to collect early morning dew to serve as water for your use. To use the soil still water method, you need to find plastic sheet, some stones and a container to collect the water.

When you get the items, you need to dig a hole in the soil; the hole should be dug directly above trees with big branches. When you are done making the hole, you then place the container inside the hole, and place leaves all around the container. After that, use the thin plastic sheet to cover the hole then place bigger pebbles or stones on the edges of the plastic sheet to hold it in place while you place a smaller pebble in the middle of the plastic sheet. This way, dew that fall on any part of the sheet rolls to the middle and drops into the container. You can use this method to source for clean drinking water daily depending on how big your container is, or you can do this in several areas to help you collect enough water.

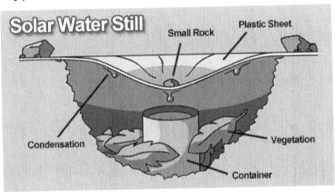

Other sources include lakes, oceans etc. Ice is also a good source of water but before you use it for water, ensure to melt it first since drinking ice can cause dehydration.

Here are some other ideas on how to collect water:

Wrap a leafy green shrub or tree branch using a plastic bag in the morning then insert a rock inside the bag to create a point where the water will collect. When the plant transpires, it produces moisture, which you will collect at the low point. As you do this, ensure the vegetation is not poisonous.

If you are near a beach (don't drink ocean water, as it is too salty and will cause dehydration), simply dig a hole that's 3-5 feet deep behind a sand dune (about 100 feet away from the waterline) then place rocks at the very bottom to ensure the sand doesn't become too active. You can then place wood around the sides if that is possible in order to ensure the walls do not cave in. You may be able to collect up to 5 gallons of water in a few hours. If the water is too salty, try moving a little farther away from the waterline. You can try the same approach in lakes; not necessarily the ocean.

How To Purify Water

Are there really ways in which you can purify the water you've collected so far, or will you have to drink germ filled dirty water just because you are stranded? The good news is that there are simple methods you can use to purify your water to make it safe for drinking and they include:

✓ Filtration With Cloth

You can use a clean cloth or wash out a dirty cloth then place it on a container to filter your water to remove debris and dirt before use.

✓ Boil The Water

This method is quite safer than the method mentioned above because it kills germs and other impurities. The best way is to boil the water first; ensure that you bring it to boil, bring down the water to cool down, and then filter with a clean piece of cloth. Ensure to aim for 10 minutes of consistent boil.

✓ Water Purification Tablet

If you're lucky enough to have a purification tablet in your survival kit, it will make the whole process easier; all you need is to drop the required quantity inside your drinking water and allow it to purify the water.

Tip: If you had packed the water purification supplies that we discussed earlier, you shouldn't have no problem in purifying water. But if you are short of supplies, boiling will be your next best option.

After water, the next thing on our discussion is food. How can you scout for food when you are in the wild when all your supplies are depleted? We will learn how to do that in the next chapter.

Sourcing For Food

Food should be the next important item on your list; remember you cannot live for so long without food. And obviously, you cannot let yourself starve when there are wild animals that you can hunt, fruits to gather and wild veggies to live on. The best options that will be at your disposal at this time for sourcing for food include; hunting, foraging, setting traps for animals and fishing. Unfortunately, if you don't have the right skill, you will die in your quest to finding food since you may eat poisonous plants or not have the skill for catching animals. I will discuss these points individually:

✓ Fishing For Survival

Some basic items you will need to construct equipment for fishing include; bamboo which you can easily get around the bushland; knife, Paracord or twine, fishing hook and bait. Here is how to fish:

- Fishing Method One

For this method, you will construct fishing equipment that has prongs and use it for fishing. You will need a bamboo, knife and a Paracord. Cut a sizeable bamboo stick from the bush land, cut the edge to look like prongs. Use a twine to separate the prongs to stand apart; the prongs should be four in number. Find a good standing spot on the river or stream, preferably on top of a stone. Once a fish comes within your range, jab it with the prongs. If you jab hard enough, the fish should die instantly.

- Fishing Method Two

This is more like the conventional fishing method you use; you need a fishing line, hook, Paracord and bait to use this method. Get a fishing line or cut down a bamboo stick, get your Paracord and tie it on the edge of your fishing line then add your fishing hook and place bait on the hook. Lower the hook inside the water then once a fish comes to eat from the hook, draw out the hook from the water quickly. This method requires much patience, but it also means that you won't be soiling the water with blood from the fish which is the case with the first method.

✓ Tips For Foraging

I mentioned earlier that you need to source for your own food to supplement the supply in your pantry bag and that means you will have to do some foraging. Foraging has to do with scouting for food from the wild. Through foraging, you can discover many delicious foods that will sustain you through the period of emergency. One disadvantage of foraging is that you can get poisoned while trying out new food especially if you don't have prior knowledge on foraging in the wild. Here are some helpful tips to help you while foraging:

1. Stick With Familiar Food

Although the major reason behind foraging is to explore and discover new food in your environment, you need to restrict your foraging to food that you are familiar with simply because although many edible foods can be food in the area, there are also many poisonous foods. Sticking to the food you are familiar with may restrict the essence of foraging, but it will also reduce your chances of getting poisoned. The last thing you want is having to deal with poison when you are out in the wild.

2. Go Easy With Unfamiliar Food

I mentioned earlier that it is advisable to stick to foods you are familiar with, but if you must go beyond that range, then you have to take just a small portion to see its effect on your body before you make it a part of your everyday meal.

3. Do Not Harvest All At Once

After you find edible foods that are nutritious to your body, you need to apply self-control and harvest the food bit by bit to ensure that it will last longer. You can even take it a step further to plant the seed, or stem of the food to produce more food for you especially if you are going to stay in that environment for a long time or indefinitely.

4. Eat Only What A Bear Can Eat

I was taught this slogan on one of my camping trips years ago, and I think it can be applicable for foraging during an emergency. The 'Eat Only what a bear can eat' simply means that if a bear cannot eat the meal, then it is not good for your body. Bears are known to eat fruits like berries and fishes; you can avoid poisoning by sticking to this principle.

5. Avoid Foraging In The Dark

No matter how adventurous you think you are, always avoid going out to find food at night if you are stranded in a desert or bush land because foraging at night will expose you to danger like getting devoured by wild animals or getting lost on the way. Always stick to daytime foraging.

Tips On How To Identify Edible Food During Foraging

Is there any particular test you can apply that will help you identify edible food when you're foraging? Yes, there are some quick tests you can use to identify edible food from poisonous food. The two popular tests for identifying edible food are the Contact Poisonous test and the mouth testing. Let's look at each of these separately.

1. *The Contact Poisonous Test*

This type of test is done by placing some parts of the seed or leaf on your skin for several minutes. If you have a burning sensation or you feel itchy on that spot, then it means that the food is a very poisonous plant. Three minutes is enough to carry out this particular test. If you have any reactions to any plant, leave the plant and continue checking other plants in the area.

2. *The Mouth Testing*

This test is actually riskier than the initial test, but much more proficient. Also, note that you have to follow the instructions to the latter to avoid food poisoning. To start this test, you have to stop eating or drinking for at least 8 hours prior to the time you will perform the test. The first step in this test is to place the leaf or the edible part of the plant on your lip for 3 minutes. If you experience a burning sensation, itching or tingling, then discard the plant immediately. If you don't experience such, then continue with the second stage. In the second stage, you proceed to place the leaf or edible part of the plant inside your mouth and hold it in place for 15 minutes. During this period, try not to swallow to avoid ingesting the plant in case it turns out to be a poisonous plant. While in your mouth, if you feel any itching, burning sensation, bitter test or tingling, you have to spit out the food and rinse your mouth immediately. If on the other hand you don't experience such, then move to the third and final stage which is chewing the food (i.e. the amount in your mouth) and swallowing. You need to stay for at least 3 hours after you swallow. If you feel any burning sensation during that period, then you have to induce vomiting immediately. You can induce vomiting by placing your finger deep inside your throat, after which you drink some water.

Hunting And Setting Traps For Survival

You need to hunt for or set traps for a bush game to get meat for your meals. I prefer setting traps to hunting because hunting requires the use of much energy and you are not advised to exhaust your energy on hunting for animals when you can simply set traps. There are many ways to set traps for animals, and one of them includes digging shallow holes for smaller games. Once the animal falls into the hole, it will find it difficult to escape thus making it easy to kill it. When using this method, ensure that you don't dig the hole on the way you usually take.

Another method is to set a trap with three pegged sticks.

How To Set A Trap With Three Pegged Stick

Get two sticks the size of your arm and drive them into the ground. Carve out a small peg on each stick. The sticks should be parallel to each other and at least two feet apart.

Drive a third stick into the ground; the stick should be 2 feet apart from the other sticks, but should be in a position to form a triangle

Use a wire to tie a small stick under the peg of the 2 parallel sticks

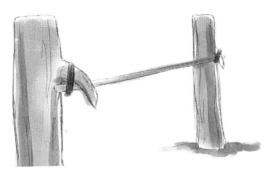

Get a long wire or cord, and tie on a sapling branch. The wire should be at least 6 to 12 inches long.

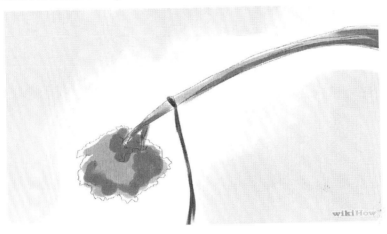

Attach a small stick on the end of the wire or cord and place the stick under the stick as can be seen in the image below

Place a trigger stick between the peg and a smaller stick on the wire or cord

Tie a noose under the trigger system and place your bait. The noose will shoot into the air with the trigger stick once an animal enters inside it.

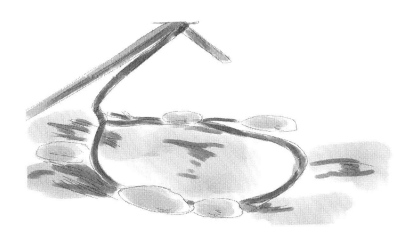

Setting Up A Survival Shelter

After you're done making provisions for water and food, the next thing on your agenda should be setting up a shelter to protect yourself from harsh weather conditions and wild animals. Although the shelter you will be setting up will not be anything close to your home, since it is an emergency situation, a survival shelter will give you the needed protection.

Items Needed To Set Up A Survival Shelter

In order to set up your survival shelter, you need to have the following items in place:

- Bamboo sticks or any other strong stick

- A sharp knife

- Twines, vines or preferable Paracord

How To Set Up A Survival Shelter

There are many ways to set up a survival shelter, but for an emergency, you can use the procedure below to set up a temporary shelter.

✓ Find A Clear Ground

You need to find an open space or a ground space without stumps; you can actually clear the ground around you to make an open space.

✓ Gather Sticks

Besides setting up the survival shelter, you will need to gather sticks to also make a fireplace. You can use this time and work on both tasks. For your fire, you need smaller and very dry sticks, but for your survival shelter, you will need to get stronger and bigger sticks.

✓ Set Up The Sticks

You need to set up the sticks to make your shelter. If the weather is too cold or you are not sure of the type of wild animals in the area, you may need to lay some sticks on top of each other to lift your shelter off the ground a bit.

After that, place the other sticks on the ground in a slanting manner to enable the sticks on one roll to touch the ones on the opposite. Continue mounting more sticks until you get to the desired length for your shelter.

Place a long stick across the slanted sticks and use a twine or the Paracord to hold them together.

Spread your emergency blanket or plastic sheeting on top of the sticks to serve as the roof; remember to create your entrance. If for any reason you don't have an emergency blanket or plastic sheeting, you can collect leaves and place on the sticks and use another set of sticks to help prevent them from blowing off when the weather gets windy in the night.

After setting up your survival shelter, you will need to make a fire in front of the shelter to keep wild animals away while you sleep, and to provide warmth for you when the temperature drops further at night.

How To Make A Fire Without A Matches Or Lighter

If you don't have a match or a fire lighter, you can use these alternative ways to set up fire:

✓ Bow And Stone Fire

This process is very easy; with a little practice, you can get the process perfectly. It involves using a bow and stone to produce sparks of fire. First, you need to make your bow; get a light stick that is flexible enough to bend.

Untie your shoe string or Paracord and use it to arch the stick. Simply bend the stick on both sides facing down and use the rope to hold the sides in place.

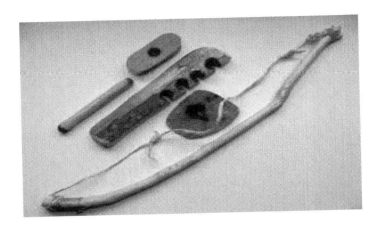

Face a wood surface and use your knife to carve a small hole on the wood;

Place some pieces of wool or tinder nest cloth to the hole; close enough to light it with fire sparks.

Place a side of the bow inside the hole and then place a stone on the end facing use; and hold it in place with your left hand and use your right hand to quickly turn the bow from side to side.

It will produce small sparks of fire to ignite the tinder.

✓ Battery And Steel Wool Fire

You can produce sparks of fire using a battery and a steel-wool. For this method, you will need a battery of at least 9 volts. Set the terminal sides of the battery (the terminals are the two metal sides that are slightly raised on the edge of your battery).

Bring a steel wool and rub both together to produce sparks of fire. Ensure that you have wool or tinder nest near that will catch the sparks to produce fire.

✓ Flint And Steel Fire

For this method, you use a flint and a piece of steel. Rub them vigorously together to produce sparks of fire but before proceeding with this method, you need to keep a small bare thread cloth nearby to catch the sparks of fire. The flint can be a small coal tar stone, and if you don't have any steel, you can use the blade of your knife as a substitute for steel.

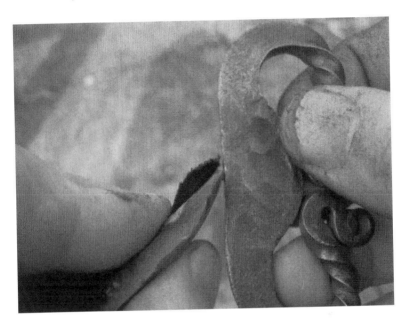

The next part will talk about how to protect yourself while in the wild.

Survival Defense Techniques

Out there in the bush land, forest or desert, you are bound to face many dangers from wild animals and other people as you try to survive. As such, you need to learn how to stay strong to survive each day until help comes your way. This is why defense techniques come in. You don't need to be a pro athlete to be able to protect yourself from dangers in the wild. Here are some of the defense techniques to help you stay alive:

✓ Dish Out Lethal Blow

You can overpower an enemy by throwing a lethal blow on the enemy. Before using this method, you have to ensure that you can easily overpower the enemy with the blow, and when throwing the blow, you have to put much energy into it. Strike with full force as though your life depends on that single blow you give, and also aim for vulnerable parts of the body like the eyes. A lethal blow can either kill the enemy or destabilize them for some time and give you enough time to escape. Also, if you are close to the enemy, you can use your elbow to strike instead of your fist; an elbow blow is more lethal than a blow with your fist.

✓ Strike With A Knife

Always ensure that you have a small sharp knife with you wherever you go. You can use the knife to strike the enemy. The knife wound may not kill the enemy at the spot, but it will give you ample time to escape. Aim for the jugular bone or the abdomen when using a knife.

✓ Claw Your Finger

If you are caught unawares by your enemy in an attack, you can defend yourself by using your nails to claw at the enemy's eyes. Once you get your target, you should be able to destabilize your enemy for awhile because no living thing can continue an attack when its eyes are hurting.

✓ Find A Distraction

Another self-defense method you can apply is the method of distraction. Find a way to distract your enemy momentarily while you strike. You can throw a stick or stone to another direction to get your enemy's eyes away from you for the moment, then take the opportunity to deal a lethal blow.

How To Outsmart Wildlife

You have to master how to outsmart wildlife in the bush land because most of the animals in the wild are actually intelligent and even faster than the fastest Olympic sprinter so running away is not just an option here for you. You can apply the following tricks to outsmart wildlife in the open.

✓ *Climb The Nearest Tree*

If you are being pursued by a wild animal, you can opt to climb any tree closest to you. Most wild animals don't know how to climb. Additionally, the good thing is that they will probably get tired waiting for you to come down. But keep in mind that this trick doesn't work for all wild animals.

✓ *Set Line Traps*

You can set a strong line trap on the pathway that the wild animals mostly use. All you need to do is to use a Paracord, and tie it from one tree trunk to another. A Paracord is very strong to trip large animals and also too tiny for any animal to see it. This will give you time to think of a good escape route before the animal regains balance.

✓ *Play Dead*

This may be the best option you have to outsmart most wild animals. Most wild animals don't eat dead meat. As such, you can outsmart them by remaining very still while they sniff you. If the animal stiffs for a short time and you remain absolutely still, it will walk away.

Thank you again for downloading this book!

I hope this book was able to help you to understand how to stay alive in the wild.

The next step is to implement what you have learnt.

Finally, if you enjoyed this book, would you be kind enough to leave a review for this book on Amazon?

Click here to leave a review for this book on Amazon!

Thank you and good luck!

Book 2
SURVIVAL

20 Advanced Strategies for Survival in Any Situation

Introduction

I want to thank you and congratulate you for downloading the book, *"SURVIVAL: 20 Advanced Strategies for Survival in Any Situation"*.

This book contains 20 actionable strategies that will help you stay alive in any survival situation.

When disaster strikes, everyone affected goes into panic (or survival) mode. If you've watched any movie involving a catastrophe, you know that when resources are scarce and hope is in limited supply, anyone can be your worst enemy. Whatever you do or don't do has to be in the best interests of your survival. So unless you are willing to die for someone, you must learn how to make it on your own without a second thought.

Nonetheless, you also have to come to terms with the fact that you just don't want to end up being the only survivor. There is beauty in knowing that you made it out of a survival situation with some people.

But as I said, you don't want to be a liability to whoever wants to survive. The more knowledgeable you are about how to survive in the situation, the more indispensable you become to everyone out there. That's why they will be willing to go to great lengths to make sure that you stay alive if they are to have any hope of survival because to them, you are like a compass in the middle of nowhere; if they lose you, they lose direction and their chances of surviving also diminishes.

In simple terms, what you know can keep you and everyone else who is with you alive. You can call the shots when there are disputes because you are the person with all the knowledge and can lead people throughout the survival period. Is that what you are looking for? Well, if that's it, then this book will give you advanced strategies that will help you stay alive under whichever circumstance.

Thanks again for downloading this book, I hope you enjoy it!

Table of Contents

Introduction

Navigating Your Way Through The Wilderness

   Using The Moon

   #1. To Find South Or North

   #2. To Find East – West

   Using The North Star

   #3. To Find North

   #4. Navigating By The Sun

Signaling

   #5.Targeted Signals

     Signal mirror

     The Signal Fire

     The Tree Torch

     Clothe And Rag Signals

Performing First Aid In The Wild

Performing First Aid In The Wild

   #6. Major Injuries

     Bleeding

     Fractures

     Dislocation

     Concussions

   #7.Minor Injuries

     Sprains

     Heat Exhaustion

Sun Stroke

Muscle Cramps

Burns

Blisters

Headaches

Frostbite

#8.Others

Stopped Breathing

Shock

#9.Animal related injuries

Snake Bites

Stings

#10.Hypothermia

#11. Hyperthermia

Essential Survival Skills

#12. Making Rope

#13. Making Knives

Knives From Rock

Knives From Metal

Knives From Bone

Knives From Wood

#14. Staff

#15. Club

Simple Club

Weighted Club

Sling Club

#16. Making A Spear

#17. Making A Throwing Stick

Throwing A Rabbit Stick

#18. Making A Quick Bow Stick

Finding A String

#19. Making An Arrow Tip

#20. Bola

Preparing Fish And Game For Cooking And Storing

Fish

Snakes

Birds

Skinning & Butchering game

The Psychological Aspect Of Wilderness Survival

Conclusion

This book is a follow up to the book "SURVIVAL: A Beginners Guide to Survive" so we will not discuss the basics. Instead, we will get straight to discussing strategies that will increase your chances of survival by a big margin. You can search for the book on Amazon. Let's get started with the strategies.

Navigating Your Way Through The Wilderness

When stranded in the wild, one of the most significant tools you can ever dream to have is a compass. What is the main purpose of a compass? Well, simple; you need a compass to capture accurate bearings and establish a direction using those bearings, or to tell you where North, East, West, and South are.

Well, when it comes to navigation, people are always concerned about bearings first, which is often the wrong approach. Taking bearings can be crucial to ascertain your position, to travel towards a certain feature, or to move through a featureless landscape. However, the most important thing to keep in mind when navigating using a compass is to know which way is South, and which is North, and then use this information to set your map accordingly. But that is neither here nor there.

Today, we are going back to the basics; to the ways of our ancestors – how to navigate through the wilderness without a compass, or, as the experts like to call it – celestial navigation. There are several broad ways of finding direction without a compass. We will look at three of these:

1. Using the moon as the reference point

2. Using the north star

3. Using the sun

Using The Moon

#1. To Find South Or North

You can use the moon to find north or south direction, except for a couple of nights every month. Since the moon does not produce its own light, it reflects the light from the sun, thus indicating the position of the sun.

A general rule of thumb

If the moon is crescent, just draw an imaginary line touching the tips of the "horns" to the horizon. Where the line ends is roughly North for the s. hemisphere and South for the n. hemisphere.

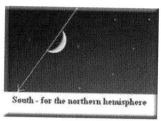

South - for the northern hemisphere

#2. To Find East – West

The moon can also be used to come up with a general east – west direction. If it rises before sunset, then the illuminated side faces west, and if it rises after midnight, then the lighted side is facing east.

Why?

Our earth rotates on its own axis to produce day & night, while the moon revolves around the earth, taking about 1 month to complete a moon phase cycle. In this time, we see different scopes of the moon from the earth, but when it is standing between the sun and the earth, it appears invisible. Then, as it travels away from the shadow of the earth at around sunset, the sun, which is in the western position, illuminates it. After midnight, it has already reached the other side of our planet, and we can see it as the eastern sunlight casts a gleam on it.

Using The North Star

#3. To Find North

Every wilderness traveler in the Northern hemisphere should be familiar with how to find the North Star. Navigation using the stars is an ancient skill that still comes in handy today, when the sky is clear.

The North Star or the Pole star determines the location of north, wherever you are in the northern hemisphere. While it is not very bright, it maintains the same position in the sky.

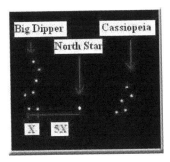

To find the North Star, Cassiopeia (W-shaped) and the Big Dipper are useful. These two constellations are always on the move, but they remain visible during a clear night. Their position is usually determined by the geographical location, date, and time. The reason why stars seem to be moving across the sky is the rotation of the Earth around its axis. To locate north:

*Look for the Big Dipper first by following the end of the cup 5x its length towards a relatively bright star. This is the North Star.

*To ascertain that it is actually the North Star, find Cassiopeia. The Pole star usually sits halfway between the Big Dipper and Cassiopeia.

#4. Navigating By The Sun

The sun is the simplest and most significant tool you can use to navigate through the wilderness without a compass and map. The sun rises in the east and sets in the west. At noon, when it is at its highest point, it will be either in the north (southern hemisphere) or south (northern hemisphere). In winter, shadows will be noticeably long because the sun will be lower in the sky.

Pockets are commonly trusted and used to find north and south directions, but the apparent simplicity of using this method may provide a wrong impression of its accuracy, as it can lead to an error of up to 20 degrees. Accurate results will require you to have a table of the direction of the sun, which you probably won't be carrying, unless you are a committed natural navigator. In any case, there are certain instances where you may obtain fairly correct directions.

Some general rules of thumb

*Only use in latitudes 40 to 60 degrees south or north of the equator, as shown in the picture below.

*The closer you get to the equator, the lower the accuracy of this method becomes.

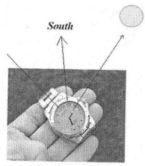

northern hemisphere

With the hour hand facing directly towards the sun, bisect the angle between 12 o'clock and the hour hand, with the imaginary line running north/south. To ascertain which end is south, keep in mind that the sun always rises in the east, is due south at noon, and sets in the west (for the N. hemisphere).

On the other hand, if you're in the S. hemisphere, point the 12 o'clock mark towards the sun, and bisect the angle between the 12 o'clock mark and the hour hand. Keep in mind the sun is due north at noon in the southern hemisphere.

Signaling

For all the preparation and planning you do to survive, the irony is that, all you actually want to do is go home. Signaling can be influential in getting you there. While setting up shelter and the what-nots are significant, once you have established immediate safety, you need to prepare your signals. And since you can never be too sure when a possible rescuer will come your way, you need to be prepared to signal at all times. Here are some techniques you can use for signaling.

#5.Targeted Signals

These signals need to be heard or seen by a target, for instance, someone in a boat, in a plane, or on foot, in order to be effective. Some are ready to use, while for others, you'll need to create yourself.

When using a visual signal to attract a passing aircraft, position it in a flat, vivid area on the highest terrain available. Keep in mind that an aircraft will likely not land right away. Look for the pilot's acknowledgement by flashing lights, dipping the aircraft's wings, dropping a message, or flying low. So how do you signal? Here are a few ways to do that:

Signal mirror

One way you can get attention is to reflect the sun's rays to distant objects, like a helicopter or airplane, using a mirror, which can reflect light up to 50 miles away on an open plane. It's more effective to signal at a distant aircraft than one that's just above you because the pilot cannot see you from directly above.

There are specially designed signaling mirrors that are made with a sighting hole at the center. However, you can use any shiny surface, like a knife blade, watch, or a compass, if you have one. Direct the reflection to the distant target until you get a response.

The Signal Fire

You must ensure that you build this in an open space, and watch your timing. You need to have set the signal fire when an aircraft passes overhead. Maintain the signal fire after lighting it, just in case the pilot tries to communicate with you.

The target will probably spot the smoke the most during the day, so you'll want to have as many items as possible that can create more of it. These include plastic and rubber, which produce black smoke, and green (fresh) boughs and branches that produce white smoke. Punky wood or moss can also be effective.

If possible, go for black smoke because this will likely not be mistaken for a campfire. In any case, smoke will work well on clear and calm days. Clouds, snow, rain, and wind shield or disperse smoke, significantly reducing its chances of being seen. Either way, you will not need the smoke at night, since the flame will be easily visible from above.

How to make a signal fire

*Start by creating a tripod of 3 trees.

*If you have an extra rope, form a platform by weaving it across the base, and then fill it with dry materials like birch bark. Place smoke-producing materials at the top, such as plastic, rubber, punky wood, or damp moss.

*Light the signal fire when a plane approaches.

The Tree Torch

This is a slight variation of the signal fire that involves setting one tree on fire. Although the most effective trees to use are dead, standing trees, you can also use live trees, especially those that bear sap. The thin bark of paper birch trees also light easily.

To create a tree torch, put dry wood at the lower branches, and set them on fire. The flame should flare upwards and ignite the overhead leaves. When making a tree torch, make sure the tree is isolated to avoid starting a forest fire!

Clothe And Rag Signals

One other way you can attract attention is to wear bright colored clothes that stand out from your surroundings (for instance, fluorescent orange). If there is no risk of them being blown away or getting wet, drape some of them on close by branches. In addition, wrap a brightly colored clothing or rag at your shelter.

Ground Signals

The best way to make ground signals is to choose an open space that can spotted easily from above. Keep in mind that things are significantly smaller from an aerial view, so size means everything.

There are several ways you can take advantage of the orange garbage bags you've packed in your survival kit – they make great ground signals because they will usually be in significantly contrast with the earth tones. Place them flatly on the ground in an open area, and use rocks to hold them in place. However, if these are not available, try using aluminum foil, orange surveyor's tape, or anything reflective or bright. You can also spell out HELP or SOS on the ground, but this can require a lot of labor. If you don't have the energy or materials to do this, a large X or V should be effective.

On the other hand, if your kit does not have the necessary tools to make a signal, natural materials can also work well. Use branches, seaweed, brush, logs, or rocks designed in words or any noticeable marking. If none of these materials are available, you can also make a signal by burning or clearing away bushes and other ground cover.

Performing First Aid In The Wild

When you are stranded in the wilderness, anything can happen anytime, and a first aid kit may really come in handy. In all cases, appropriate clothing, cleanliness, and a good diet will reduce your risk of harmful situations.

You can usually avoid infections, diseases, and even insect bites by maintaining a proper diet. It goes without saying that you need to bathe every day, but if this is not an option, make sure that you wash your hands regularly. You can make soap using animal fat or ashes, or by boiling the internal bark of a pine tree. Mash the edge of a green twig to make a toothbrush.

In case of an accident, it will be up to you to take responsibility of the situation. The exact series of events to follow when dealing with such a circumstance is:

*Stay calm to allow quiet and efficient first aid treatment

*Lay down and keep patient warm. Do not move until you've determined the extent of your injuries.

*Stop any breathing

*Check for injuries, breaks, fractures, and cuts on the spine, neck, or head

*Unless it is absolutely necessary, avoid removing clothing

*Prepare a conducive living area where there is food, heat, and shelter

So how do you move on after an injury? Well, this will depend on the severity of the injury. Let's discuss this in detail:

#6. Major Injuries

Bleeding

*Lift the wounded region above the heart.

*Apply pressure using sphagnum moss, dried seaweed, clean cloth, or gauze.

*If bleeding does not stop, apply pressure at the pulse area between the heart and the injured area.

*If bleeding persists, apply a tourniquet between the heart and the injury.

*Once you've controlled the bleeding, use a disinfectant (if available) to wash the wound and apply bandages and a dressing.

Fractures

A fracture can be either open (compound) or closed (simple). Signs of a fracture include:

*A grating sound or sensation when the injured area is moved

*Inability to apply pressure on the area without feeling pain

*The area may be deformed

*Pain

Start treatment as follows:

*If not sure, assume the injury is a fracture

*Immobilize the joints below and above the fracture

*If there's a risk of the facture penetrating the skin, you may need to apply traction to reverse the deformity

*Make sure you've padded your splints, checking the splint ties regularly to ensure they do not prevent circulation

*Use a clean dressing to cover any open wound before splinting

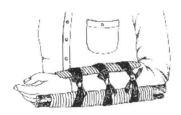

Dislocation

This occurs when the ligaments close to a joint break, allowing the bone to move from its socket. Unless you're a trained professional, it is ill-advised to treat a dislocation as it may lead to permanent damage. Just use a sling or other tool to support the affected extremity, and control the pain using aspiring or other similar drugs.

Concussions

These are usually followed by an outflow of watery blood from the ears or nose, as well as vomiting, headache, and convulsions. Keep the patient warm, give a painkiller on a regular basis, and give the body some time to rest and heal.

#7.Minor Injuries

Sprains

Apply water on the affected area for the first day, and then let it stay for a day when the swelling has decreased. You should splint the sprain and immobilize it until all the pain has disappeared.

Heat Exhaustion

This is very common when there's insufficient water. The body becomes salt-depleted and dehydrated, leading to a weak and rapid pulse, faintness, nausea, and cold & clammy skin in some cases. Treatment involves salt & liquid tablets, and plenty of rest.

Sun Stroke

This usually occurs because of too much sun exposure. The body becomes inflamed, providing excessive blood to your circulatory system. This can lead to dizziness, headache, rapid pulse, and hot, flushed face. Heat stroke inhibits the natural ability of the body to cool itself, and can cause death if not addressed quickly.

Get the patient under a shade, and remove any restrictive clothes to facilitate evaporation. Find water to pour on the body, even if it is contaminated, and allow it to evaporate from the skin. You can also fan the victim to speed up the cooling process. The victim should then take water in small amounts after every few minutes, as large amounts can cause vomiting.

Muscle Cramps

These occur when muscle accumulates too much lactic acid, or loses salt through perspiration. You can treat by stretching, deep breathing, and resting, and restoring the salt balance right away.

Burns

These are usually accompanied by shock. Provide a pain reliever instantly – cover gauze with Vaseline and apply on the affected area. Bandage, and provide the patient with more drinking water than usual.

Blisters

These are common, and are usually caused by ill-fitting footwear. Remove your socks and boots, and cover the affected area with an adhesive tape. If you have to open a blister, wash the region thoroughly first before injecting the edge of the blister with a sterilized needle. Apply disinfectant and secure with a bandage.

Headaches

These are common in the mountains, and can occur when you take large amounts of water without ingesting salt tablets, your brain tissue swells after sweating excessively for a few days, experience "water intoxication" or constipation, tension in the neck, and have insufficient eye protection. You can also use aspirin to alleviate the pain, although you should determine the source of the headache to avoid further discomfort.

Frostbite

This happens when the tissues of a region, usually the face, finger, or toes, are frozen from either high wind or direct contact with the elements. When dealing with first degree frostbite, the area can turn numb, white, and cold. When heated, it turns red and appears like a first-degree burn.

Second degree frost bites, on the other hand, form a blister after warming.

Third degree is associated with a loss of some tissues and skin, as well as gangrene and dark skin.

Fourth degree frostbite leads to irreparable damage. The part can remain lifeless and cold, and cause a part of the affected area to tear off.

You can easily avoid frostbite by wearing adequate clothing. You can treat superficial frostbite by cupping your hands and blowing against the affected part.

#8.Others

Stopped Breathing

Start mouth-to-mouth resuscitation immediately. With the patient on his or her back, proceed with the following steps:

*Lift his/her neck to open the airway and tilt head backwards

* Pinch the nostrils to stop air leakage

*Put your mouth fully around the patient's mouth, and start blowing as you watch out for chest expansion

*Remove your mouth, and listen for air exiting the victim's lungs. Wait for the chest to fall, and if it doesn't, look for an airway blockage.

Do these steps repeatedly for about twelve to fifteen times per minute.

Shock

This is when all your body processes become depressed, and can be associated with any injury, no matter how small. Shock can be intensified by such factors as pain, cold, and hemorrhage. When in shock, you may feel weak, and eventually faint. Your skin becomes clammy and cold, and your pulse rapid and weak. In fact, the shock can be more threatening than the actual injury. Here's how to prevent and manage shock:

*If there are any injuries: stop bleeding, restore breathing, and treat fractures and breaks

*If there are no chest or head injuries, lie the patient on his or her back with the legs higher than the chest and head to facilitate blood circulation to the lungs, heart, brain, and other significant organs.

*Lift the upper body if there are any severe chest and head injuries. For chest injuries, let the injured side stay elevated on the side to help the uninjured lung function properly.

*If the patient loses consciousness, lie him or her face down on the floor to prevent chocking on the tongue, vomit, or blood.

*Keep patient warm and sheltered

#9.Animal related injuries

Snake Bites

In case you encounter a snake, you should ease back slowly. It is very rare for a snake bite to cause death, and you can actually stay for up to 8 hours untreated. After an attack:

*Keep the victim calm, and reassure him/her that the bite can be treated effectively. Restrict movement, keeping the affected part right below heart level to limit the flow of the venom. Movement only makes the venom to circulate faster.

*Clean the area where the there is a bite to remove any venom that may have been left on the surface.

*Take off any constricting items such as rings because the bitten area may swell. Construct a light splint to minimize mobility of the area.

*In case the affected area starts to change color or swell, the snake was likely poisonous.

*Monitor vital signs – blood pressure, breathing rate, pulse, temperature. In case of shock, lay the person flat on the ground, lift their feet up, and cover them with a blanket

*If you cannot get medical attention within 30 minutes, wrap a bandage tightly 2-4 inches above the bite (towards the heart) to reduce the flow of venom. Ensure to wind around and move up then down over the bite and then past it as you move towards the hand or foot. The idea here is to make it tight enough to allow minimal blood flow. You don't want it too tight to cause tissue damage when you cut off circulation. Besides, if the bandage is too tight, the patient will tend to move the limb reflexively and this is likely to move the venom around, something which you are trying to avoid. You can immobilize the limb using a sling or splint to ensure that there is minimal movement.

In addition, keep the patient on bed rest while the bite site is lower than the heart for about 24-48 hours.

Tip: Draw a circle around the affected area if possible. The idea here is to help you to track improvement or worsening of the site clearly.

If you had a snake bite kit in your survival bag, simply place the suction device over the bite to help draw venom out of the wound. Ensure to leave it on for about 10 minutes. If you do this fast enough, you can remove up to 30% of the venom.

Only use this if absolutely necessary:

Make an incision (which is no longer than six millimeters and not deeper than three millimeters) over each puncture ensuring to cut deep enough to enlarge the fang opening. As you do this, be careful not to go past the second layer of the skin. Then place a suction cup over the bite so that you can have a good vacuum seal. Try to suction the bite site for about 3-4 times. If suction device is not available, you can use your mouth but ensure that you don't have open sores (venom is transferred through blood and open tissues and not the digestive tract). Ensure to spit the envenomed blood out then rinse your mouth with water.

Note: Ensure to move quickly (within a minute) to administer some of venom removal strategies above if you really want to get as much venom out as possible.

Stings

Unless you have a severe allergy, bee stings are relatively harmless. Just remove the stinger and apply disinfectant. You can usually remove the stinger by scraping up & down from the affected area using a knife blade or fingernail.

Being stung by a scorpion or spider is more serious, and there is little you can do for treatment, unless you have an antivenin by chance. In any case, watch out for anaphylaxis, and then clean and dress the affected area. In addition, treat yourself or the victim for diarrhea, vomiting, and shock, should they appear. Spider bites cause ulcerated areas that are stubborn to heal. Cover the ulcers to avoid infection.

#10.Hypothermia

When your body's temperature falls down to such a level that your vital organs are unable to function, this is known as exposure sickness or hypothermia. Hypothermia usually develops rapidly, and is brought about by cold, windy/wet weather that chills your body at a faster rate than it can generate heat. Lack of proper clothing and energy producing food will increase the rate at which you'll be affected by hypothermia. Always make a point of packing extra clothing, if possible. Symptoms include:

*Feeling cold

*Uncontrollable numbness and shivering

*Rigorous shivers. Your mind slows down and begins to wander

*Rigorous shivering stops and muscles start to stiffen and become uncoordinated

*Respiration and pulse slows down

*Victim stops responding and loses consciousness

*The part of your brain that controls the lungs and heart stops functioning

Treatment should be quick and proficient:

*Move victim away from the elements, and into a sheltered area

*Replace wet clothes with dry ones

*Bind warm rocks, and put them near the victim

*Make sure the victim does not lose consciousness

*Give him/her a warm drink (non-alcoholic)

*Exhale warm air close to the victim's nose and mouth

#11. Hyperthermia

This occurs when your body becomes overheated because of increased air temperature, reflected or solar radiation, excess bulk or a low fitness level, or poorly ventilated clothing.

Symptoms include:

*Presence of heat cramps, which should be treated by transferring the patient to a sheltered area and providing water & salt tablets

*Heat exhaustion, which is accompanied by such symptoms as vomiting, nausea, blurred vision, clammy skin, fainting, dizziness, and headache. Treatment is similar to heat cramps.

*Heat stroke, in which the patient's perspiration will be significantly diminished, become aggressive or apathetic, have full pulse, and a hot & flushed face. For this, cool the patient as quickly as you can, being particularly mindful of the chest, neck, and head. If the body's temperature continues

rising, it may lead to convulsions, delirium, unconsciousness, and eventually death.

You can avoid hyperthermia by steering away from strenuous activity during hot days, wearing a hat and loose clothing, drinking plenty of fluids, and taking salt tablets.

Essential Survival Skills

Like your early ancestors, you can be able to harness the great qualities of Ingenuity and adaptability that will come in handy in a survival situation.

#12. Making Rope

*Find some fibrous material, like the yucca plant husks, and split them into strands.

*Twist every piece in a clockwise motion between 2 fingers, and then twist the 2 pieces in an anticlockwise direction.

*Collect enough strands to make the rope as thick as necessary. Rough up or roll the strands together to acquire separate pieces.

*When you are done, the final product will be a strong rope you can use for several purposes.

#13. Making Knives

Knives From Rock

You can be able to design a knife-edge using rock that can be effective in getting you through most situations.

*Look for a hard, suitable rock, and hammer it using a larger rock

*With the right material, you can use a split rock effectively as a scraping or cutting edge, which can be sharpened by rubbing against another rock.

*Keep your rudimentary knife safe, as it will have many uses.

Knives From Metal

The biggest challenge here is finding a metal that is the right shape and size.

*Sharpen the blade and point by rubbing the metal against a rigid surface.

*You will need a handle for your hands' protection. Use rope, cloth, or tape for this purpose.

Knives From Bone

Bones are more effective at puncturing than scraping or cutting, since they don't have the capability to hold an edge.

*Place the bone on a rigid object, and strike it with a heavy material to shatter it. Pick a fittingly pointy bit from the shattered pieces.

*Rub the bone against a rough rock to refine its shape.

Knives From Wood

Wood can be very difficult to form a sharp edge, so they are mostly used for scraping and puncturing.

*Look for a piece of hardwood, roughly 30 cm (12 inches) long and 5cm (2 inches) in diameter, with a blade of 15 cm (6 inches) in length.

*Rub the wood against a hard, rigid surface, like a rock, to shave it down

#14. Staff

*Look for a relatively straight piece of hardwood, which can reach eye level from the ground.

*Use this as a weapon, to prevent brush from affecting your eyes, to check for snakes, to help with sharp hikes. It is best to find one that's strong and thick enough to fit in your hand.

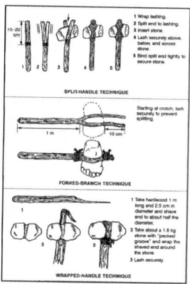

Figure 13-1. Lashing clubs.

#15. Club

These are smaller when compared to the staff, but much easier to handle.

Simple Club

This is just a simpler version of a staff, which is easier to handle since it is shorter. However, it needs to be longer in order to cause and withstand damage. The best material to use is straight-grained hardwood.

Weighted Club

This is a simple club with an attached weight at one end. You can make wrapped-handle clubs, forked-branch clubs, and split-handled clubs.

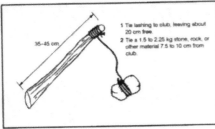

Figure 12-2. Sling club.

Sling Club

This is a weighted club with the weight hanging about four inches from the club through strong lashing that creates an impact multiplier on contact.

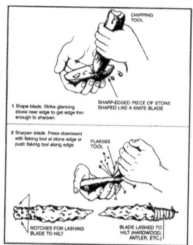

CHIPPING TOOL

SHARP-EDGED PIECE OF STONE SHAPED LIKE A KNIFE BLADE

1 Shape blade. Strike glancing blows near edge to get edge thin enough to sharpen.

2 Sharpen blade. Press downward with flaking tool at stone edge or push flaking tool along edge.

FLAKING TOOL

NOTCHES FOR LASHING BLADE TO HILT

BLADE LASHED TO HILT (HARDWOOD, ANTLER, ETC.)

Figure 12-3. Making a stone knife.

#16. Making A Spear

✓ Find the right stick

Select hardwood species such as osage, maple, locust, ash, hickory, oak, and anything else that is dense, as opposed to soft woods such as aspen, pine, and poplar that tend to break easily.

Choose a ready-to-go size that'll save you plenty of carving work.

✓ Point and bake

Carve a point at one end, and make it as sharp as you can.

Dry out the wood by passing and rotating the carved part just above a small fire. Do this until it starts looking "toasted" at the heated end.

Once you are done, rub some animal or plant oil on the pointed end, which you should sharpen again after fire hardening.

#17. Making A Throwing Stick

*Go for a heavy hardwood, like the oak, and choose a stick with a suitable angle, typically 12 to 24 inches long.

*If you can't find a stick with the desired angle, you can warp green wood. Just heat it to make it pliable, and then bend it and place the arched stick between 2 rocks until it has dried and cooled off.

*You can decide to either flatten the throwing stick or make it round. To flatten it, shape the stick like a boomerang by shaving off 2 opposite sides. This is a lot more aerodynamic and concentrates the area of impact on a smaller surface area. In any case, you should remove the bark, and smooth the surface to enhance aerodynamics.

*The shape of the throwing stick can vary significantly. It is very rare to find straight sticks, with the most common ones being Z shaped, L shaped, and V shaped.

Throwing A Rabbit Stick

For speed and accuracy, you need to practice your throwing technique.

*First, align your non-throwing arm with the target at its middle to lower section

*Slowly and continually lift up your throwing arm and back until the stick crosses your back at approximately 45 degrees.

*Bring your throwing arm forward to place it in parallel and slightly above the other arm. This will be the release point of your throwing stick.

#18. Making A Quick Bow Stick

When you need to shoot right away, you should go for a hardwood stick, which is dead & dry. Some of the options to choose from include Osage orange, locust, maple, ash, elm, and hickory.

Crafting a long bow is another trick you can use to start shooting immediately. A stave made from a dead sapling or dead branch that's 6 feet in length will be more forgiving, as compared to a shorter bow that will need to bend more in order to achieve the draw length, which could subsequently break the bow, lead the limbs flying back, and injure you.

During construction, tillering is involved to make most bows out of a single piece of wood. This is basically slimming down the wood in order for all the limbs of the bow to bend equally. It also helps provide the bow with the appropriate draw weight.

To make a quickie bow, just carve down the inner side of your bow using your handmade knife, and then scrape and/or sand the wood. However, if you are in a hurry, and there's no significant difference in the limbs' diameter, just string it up.

Finding A String

Traditionally, bowstrings are made from dried intestine strips, rawhide strips, plant fiber, and other natural substances. However, for now, you could use a 550-length cord from your pack, which should have a good diameter and enough strength to serve as a bowstring. You can use the paracord in your survival bag if you still have it.

When tying the second knot of the string to your bow, make sure the distance between the string and the grip is approximately 8 - 9 inches.

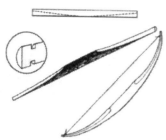

#19. Making An Arrow Tip

For this, follow the procedures we used to make a stone knife. Chert or flint is best for this. However, you can also use broken glass.

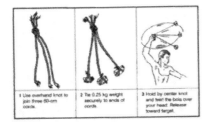

1 Use overhead knot to join three 60-cm cords.

2 Tie 0.25 kg weight securely to ends of cords.

3 Hold by center knot and twirl the bola over your head. Release toward target.

#20. Bola

This is extremely effective at capturing running game. To make it, tie 3 cords of the same length together, and attach an eight-ounce rock at the ends. Whirl from the connecting knot to your overhead, and release to your target.

Preparing Fish And Game For Cooking And Storing

When in a survival situation, it is important to know how to prepare game and fish for cooking and preserving. Improper storage or cleaning can render the game or fish inedible.

Fish

Stay away from fish that looks spoiled. It's not a guarantee that cooking it will make it edible. You may be able to determine spoiled fish by:

*Peppery or sharp taste

*Slimy, instead of wet or moist body

*Dents remain in the flesh after pressing with a thumb

*Suspicious color (scales should be vivid gray, while gills should be pink to red)

*Peculiar odor

*Sunken eyes

Eating rotten or spoiled fish may lead to paralysis, itching, vomiting, cramps, nausea, diarrhea, or a metallic sensation in the mouth. The symptoms occur suddenly, about 1 to 6 hours after ingesting. If you experience these symptoms, induce vomiting.

Fish tends to spoil quickly, especially when it's hot. Remove the gills & large blood vessels close to the spine. Catch fish that's more than ten centimeters in length.

You may decide to spear the whole fish and cook it over the flames of an open fire. However, the best way to acquire the most value is to boil it with the skin on. The oil and fats are below the skin, and when you boil the fish, you can preserve the juice for soup.

Place the fish on a ball of clay, and heat on the hot coals until the clay toughens. Break the clay ball to remove the cooked fish. You'll know when it's done if the meat flecks off. Fry or smoke the fish if you intend to keep for later. For smoking, remove the backbone and cut off the head first.

Snakes

First, cut off the head of the snake and bury it. Now, cut the body down, starting fifteen to twenty centimeters from the head.

Next, peel out the skin, and hold the body and the skin in opposite hands. Cook the snake like you would cook small game. Remove and discard the entrails. Chop the snake to small bits and then roast or boil it.

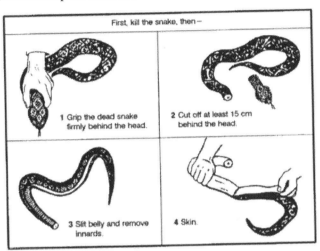

First, kill the snake, then—

1 Grip the dead snake firmly behind the head.

2 Cut off at least 15 cm behind the head.

3 Slit belly and remove innards.

4 Skin.

Birds

Once you've killed the bird, skin it or pluck out the feathers. Open its body cavity and extract its entrails, setting aside the craw, liver, and heart. Cut the feet off, and then cook the meet by roasting or boiling. When dealing with scavenger birds, be sure to boil them for at least twenty minutes to kill off parasites.

Skinning & Butchering game

Cut the animal's throat to bleed it out. If possible, do the dirty job near a stream. With the carcass placed stomach up, cut down the hide from the throat to the tail, leaving out all the sexual organs. For smaller animals, you can split it down into two by inserting two fingers beneath the hide on either side and pulling the pieces off.

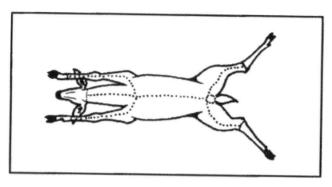

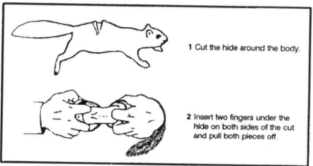

1 Cut the hide around the body.

2 Insert two fingers under the hide on both sides of the cut and pull both pieces off.

For larger animals, separate the gullet from the diaphragm, and remove the entrails from the body after cutting around the anus. Reach for the lower abdominal cavity, and pull out the lower intestine. Pinch off and cut out the urine bladder using your fingers. In case the urine spills on the meat, rinse it well to avoid contaminating the meat. Set aside the liver and heart. Cut them open and look for signs of worm infestation or other parasites. In addition, inspect the color of the liver, making sure that the color is purple or deep blue, and the surface is wet and smooth. Discard the liver if it looks diseased.

Cut through the leg, from the last cut off point, to above the foot. Pull out the hide of the carcass, splitting any necessary connective tissues. Cut off the feet and head, and then chop the meat into smaller pieces. Four-legged animals do not have any joints or bones connecting the body with the front legs. Cut off the hindquarters at the adjourning point with the body.

Cut out the ligaments near the joint, and arch it backwards to split it. Get out the large muscles lying on both sides of the spine. Divide the backbone and the ribs.

Boil the larger pieces of meat or cook them over a split. You can stew the smaller pieces, or boil them, especially those that stick to the meat after butchering, and use as broth or soup. Body organs like the kidneys, spleen, pancreas, liver, and heart can be cooked in the same manner as muscle meat. Don't be shy to eat the brain as well!

The Psychological Aspect Of Wilderness Survival
Stress and stressors

Everyone has a point in life when they have felt stressed. Stress is inevitable in the modern day, but very few stressors can compare to those that you will encounter in a survival situation. However, stress can be beneficial sometimes, regardless of the tremendous pressure it heaps on us. Stressors can prompt you to work at your peak level, providing you with the energy to utilize your strengths and work on your witnesses.

But stress can be a destructive force as well. Chronic amounts can cause distress, which can in turn change into panic. Nonetheless, the secret to overcoming a survival situation is challenging and controlling the stressor you may encounter. These are several and varied, among them being a general lack of control, loneliness & isolation, boredom & depression, negative group dynamics, fatigue, lack of knowledge, cold or heat, the environment, thirst, hunger, injury & illness, and indubitably, death.

You need to acknowledge, confront, and deal with each one of these needs. Keep in mind that when fighting for your life, it is important to rule out disadvantages. Unlike in the office, you can't sweep the problems facing you aside. In the wild, there is no procrastinating or ignoring! You deal with the problem at hand then move on to the next phase of staying alive. If you cannot do that, then you can bet that your chances of staying alive until help arrives are probably limited.

Conclusion

Thank you again for downloading this book!

I hope this book was able to help you to understand how to move past the beginner level of survival to the pro level.

The next step is to implement what you have learnt.

Welcome to the **BONUS** page!

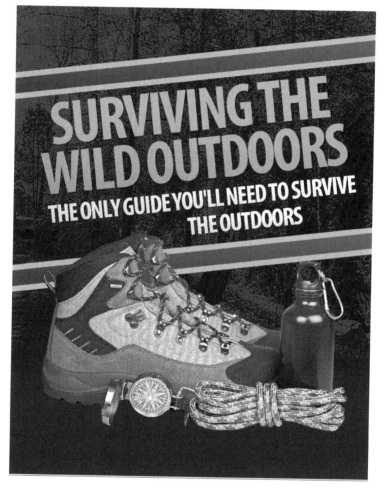

https://thetreplife.leadpages.co/survivingthewildoutdoors/?es=ml4gbyxjogba
gxf7s8ypcqbtfy47pe6t

Finally, if you feel like you got value from this book and you enjoyed it, I'd
really appreciate it if you would you be kind enough to leave a review for this
book on Amazon?

Thank you and good luck!

If you enjoyed this book check out my other titles

PREPPER

No 1 Survival Guide Book For Prepper's

SURVIVAL PANTRY

A Prepper's Guide to Storing Food and Water

Made in the USA
San Bernardino, CA
16 December 2016